M000164567

be bright
be bold
be you

Lucy Lane

summersdale

BE BRIGHT, BE BOLD, BE YOU

An Hachette UK Company
www.hachette.co.uk

Summersdale Publishers Ltd
Part of Octopus Publishing Group Limited
Carmelite House
50 Victoria Embankment
LONDON
EC4Y 0DZ
UK

www.summersdale.com

Printed and bound in China

ISBN: 978-1-78783-243-5

Substantial discounts on bulk quantities of Summersdale books are available to corporations, professional associations and other organizations. For details contact general enquiries: telephone: +44 (0) 1243 771107 or email: enquiries@summersdale.com.

To..

From..

You can, you should, and if you're brave enough to start, you will.

STEPHEN KING

Never
lose your
sparkle

If not me, who?
If not now, when?

HILLEL THE ELDER

YOU DESERVE
GREATNESS,
SO GIVE IT
TO YOURSELF.

CHIDERA EGGERUE

You've got this

If you want something done, honey, do it yourself.

REESE WITHERSPOON

MAKE BOLD
CHOICES AND
MAKE MISTAKES.
IT'S ALL THOSE
THINGS THAT ADD
UP TO THE PERSON
YOU BECOME.

ANGELINA JOLIE

Be better,
be brighter,
be bolder

When you become the image of your own imagination, it's the most powerful thing you could ever do.

RuPAUL

Be bold, be
brave enough
to be your
true self.

QUEEN LATIFAH

Inhale confidence. Exhale doubt.

WHAT WOULD
LIFE BE IF WE HAD
NO COURAGE
TO ATTEMPT
ANYTHING?

VINCENT van GOGH

IF THEY DON'T
LIKE YOU FOR
BEING YOURSELF,
BE YOURSELF
EVEN MORE.

TAYLOR SWIFT

Out with the old, in with the bold

Create what you want to create, and be free to try anything.

ROBERT DE NIRO

Find out who
you are and do
it on purpose.

DOLLY PARTON

I am
resilient,
brave,
and
strong

With confidence,
you have won
even before you
have started.

MARCUS GARVEY

IT IS CONFIDENCE
IN OUR BODIES,
MINDS AND SPIRITS
THAT ALLOWS US TO
KEEP LOOKING FOR
NEW ADVENTURES.

OPRAH WINFREY

Dream big.
Work hard.
Make it
happen.

I'M NOT IN THIS
WORLD TO LIVE
UP TO YOUR
EXPECTATIONS AND
YOU ARE NOT IN
THIS WORLD TO
LIVE UP TO MINE.

FRITZ PERLS

Don't you ever let a soul in the world tell you that you can't be exactly who you are.

LADY GAGA

The most
courageous act
is still to think for
yourself. Aloud.

COCO CHANEL

Do not wait,
the time will never
be "just right".
Start where
you stand.

GEORGE HERBERT

I'm working on myself, for myself, by myself

Failure will never overtake me if my determination to succeed is strong enough.

OG MANDINO

OUR UNIQUENESS,
OUR INDIVIDUALITY
AND OUR LIFE
EXPERIENCE
MOULDS US INTO
FASCINATING
BEINGS.

LINDA THOMPSON

Choose happy

IT DOES NOT
MATTER HOW
SLOWLY YOU GO
AS LONG AS YOU
DO NOT STOP.

CONFUCIUS

The fact that
I'm me and no one
else is one of my
greatest assets.

HARUKI MURAKAMI

Fortune favours the bold

The single greatest gift you could ever give to the world is to be exactly who you are.

JENNA MARBLES

I have a confidence about my life that comes from standing tall on my own two feet.

JANE FONDA

The
future is
bright

THERE'S SOMETHING WILDLY FREEING ABOUT SOMEONE WHO'S UNAPOLOGETIC.

MELISSA McCARTHY

IF YOU'RE
PRESENTING
YOURSELF WITH
CONFIDENCE,
YOU CAN PULL
OFF PRETTY MUCH
ANYTHING.

KATY PERRY

Chase your dreams

Wanting to
be someone else
is a waste of the
person you are.

KURT COBAIN

Be yourself.
The world worships
the original.

INGRID BERGMAN

You do you

You can reinvent yourself and learn new things whenever you want.

JONATHAN VAN NESS

SELF-LOVE HAS
VERY LITTLE TO DO
WITH HOW YOU
FEEL ABOUT YOUR
OUTER SELF.
IT'S ABOUT
ACCEPTING ALL
OF YOURSELF.

TYRA BANKS

I am
fearless

The greatest
thing in the world
is to know how to
belong to oneself.

MICHEL DE **MONTAIGNE**

Love yourself
first and everything
else falls into line.

LUCILLE BALL

Sparkle more

NOTHING CAN
DIM THE LIGHT
WHICH SHINES
FROM WITHIN.

MAYA ANGELOU

Just believe in yourself. Even if you don't, pretend that you do and, at some point, you will.

VENUS WILLIAMS

You already have what it takes

Life is too short
to be same person
every day.

STEPHANIE PERKINS

THE ONLY EXPECTATIONS I NEED TO LIVE UP TO ARE MY OWN.

MICHELLE OBAMA

Your only limit is your mind

It's only when you risk failure that you discover things.

LUPITA NYONG'O

BE WHO YOU ARE AND SAY WHAT YOU FEEL.

BERNARD M. BARUCH

Only seek
to be more
of yourself

Be what you are. This is the first step toward becoming better than you are.

JULIUS CHARLES HARE

TURN YOUR FACE
TO THE SUN AND
THE SHADOWS FALL
BEHIND YOU.

MĀORI PROVERB

One fails
forward toward
success.

CHARLES F. KETTERING

Power's not given to you. You have to take it.

BEYONCÉ

Be thankful for who you are now, but keep fighting for who you want to be

YOU BUILD
ON FAILURE.
YOU USE IT AS A
STEPPING STONE.

JOHNNY CASH

Be happy with being you. Love your flaws. Own your quirks.

ARIANA GRANDE

Own who
you are

TO BE YOURSELF
IN A WORLD THAT
IS CONSTANTLY
TRYING TO MAKE
YOU SOMETHING
ELSE IS THE GREATEST
ACCOMPLISHMENT.

RALPH WALDO EMERSON

TRANSFORMING FEAR INTO FREEDOM – HOW GREAT IS THAT?

SOLEDAD O'BRIEN

Top of my to-do list: live in the moment

Being confident
is the key to life.
Don't be afraid
to be you!

LEO HOWARD

Be sure what
you want and
be sure about
yourself.

ADRIANA LIMA

Make your heart the most beautiful thing about you

Hope lies in dreams, in imagination and in the courage of those who dare to make dreams into reality.

JONAS SALK

I'VE ALWAYS
LOVED THE IDEA
OF NOT BEING
WHAT PEOPLE
EXPECT ME TO BE.

DITA von TEESE

Be the
energy you
want to
attract

I AM NOT
A HAS-BEEN.
I AM A WILL-BE.

LAUREN BACALL

It's character traits like persistence, ambition, inquisitiveness and grit that will determine your success.

AMAL CLOONEY

Be anything but predictable

Take care
not to listen to
anyone who tells
you what you can
and can't be in life.

MEG MEDINA

I just go with the flow; I follow the yellow brick road.

GRACE JONES

The only step you will regret is the one you don't take

WHAT I AM IS
GOOD ENOUGH
IF I WOULD ONLY
BE IT OPENLY.

CARL ROGERS

I'M NOT AFRAID
OF STORMS, FOR
I'M LEARNING HOW
TO SAIL MY SHIP.

LOUISA MAY ALCOTT

Never
doubt your
worth

You are
what you do,
not what you
say you'll do.

CARL JUNG

You are your
own best friend,
the key to your
own happiness.

CHERIE LUNGHI

Don't change yourself so that other people will like you. Be yourself so that the right people will love you

Just because they disagree, doesn't mean you ain't right.

TOBA BETA

DO THE THINGS THAT INTEREST YOU AND DO THEM WITH ALL YOUR HEART.

ELEANOR ROOSEVELT

Be perfectly imperfect

YOU WERE BORN
AN ORIGINAL,
DON'T DIE A COPY.

JOHN MASON

Who you
are is what you
settle for.

JANIS JOPLIN

You
totally
can

There are
two ways of
spreading light:
to be the candle
or the mirror
that reflects it.

EDITH WHARTON

TELL ME, WHAT IS
IT YOU PLAN TO
DO WITH YOUR
ONE WILD AND
PRECIOUS LIFE?

MARY OLIVER

Imperfection is a form of freedom

The only way you're going to get through life, happily, is being yourself.

NIKKI BLONSKY

YOU MAY NOT
CONTROL ALL
THE EVENTS THAT
HAPPEN TO YOU,
BUT YOU CAN
DECIDE NOT TO
BE REDUCED
BY THEM.

MAYA ANGELOU

Don't stop until you're proud

Just when the caterpillar thought the world was over, it became a butterfly.

PROVERB

The pen
that writes your
life story must
be held in your
own hand.

IRENE C. KASSORLA

Find
beauty in
imperfection

MAYBE OTHER
PEOPLE WILL TRY
TO LIMIT ME BUT
I DON'T LIMIT
MYSELF.

JIM CARREY

YOU'RE ALWAYS
WITH YOURSELF,
SO YOU MIGHT
AS WELL ENJOY
THE COMPANY.

DIANE VON FÜRSTENBERG

Don't look back: you're not going that way

Learn to be what you are, and learn to resign with a good grace all that you are not.

HENRI-FRÉDÉRIC AMIEL

If you are happy
from within,
you are the most
beautiful person.

ILEANA D'CRUZ

Find out what sets your soul on fire and let it burn

Always be
a first-rate version
of yourself, instead of
a second-rate version
of someone else.

JUDY GARLAND

WHAT A DULL
AND POINTLESS
LIFE IT WOULD
BE IF EVERYBODY
WAS THE SAME.

ANGELINA JOLIE

The
bravest
thing you
can be is
yourself

STAND UP TO
YOUR OBSTACLES
AND DO SOMETHING
ABOUT THEM.

NORMAN VINCENT PEALE

A head full of fears has no space for dreams.

ANONYMOUS

Your willingness
to wrestle with
your demons
will cause your
angels to sing.

AUGUST WILSON

Be messy
and complicated
and afraid and show
up anyways.

GLENNON DOYLE

It's
time to
write
a new
story

No one
saves us but
ourselves.
No one can
and no
one may.

PAUL CARUS

YOU GET WHATEVER
ACCOMPLISHMENT
YOU ARE WILLING
TO DECLARE.

GEORGIA O'KEEFFE

Difficult
roads often
lead to
beautiful
destinations

EXPECT THE BEST.
PREPARE FOR THE
WORST. CAPITALIZE
ON WHAT COMES.

ZIG ZIGLAR

Either you run
the day, or the
day runs you.

JIM ROHN

Say yes
to new
adventures

Infuse your
life with action.
Don't wait for it
to happen.

BRADLEY WHITFORD

If you can't go straight ahead, you go around the corner.

CHER

You can move mountains

TO THE DOUBTERS
AND NAYSAYERS…
YOUR RESISTANCE
MADE ME STRONGER,
MADE ME PUSH
HARDER.

MADONNA

DON'T SPEND
ALL OF YOUR TIME
TRYING TO BE LIKE
SOMEONE ELSE,
BECAUSE YOU CAN
NEVER BE THEM
AND THEY CAN
NEVER BE YOU.

RAVEN-SYMONÉ

Kind heart,
fierce mind,
brave spirit

A good heart is better than all the heads in the world.

EDWARD BULWER-LYTTON

Owning up to
your vulnerabilities
is a form of strength.

LIZZO

The fears
we don't
face become
our limits.

ROBIN SHARMA

TALK TO YOURSELF LIKE YOU WOULD TO SOMEONE YOU LOVE.

BRENÉ BROWN

You are magic

You can do
whatever you
really love to do,
no matter
what it is.

RYAN GOSLING

Normal is not something to aspire to, it's something to get away from.

JODIE FOSTER

Be brave
with
your life

HE WHO HAS
OVERCOME HIS
FEARS WILL
TRULY BE FREE.

ARISTOTLE

Cherish forever what makes you unique, 'cuz you're really a yawn if it goes.

BETTE MIDLER

Enjoy the beauty of becoming

We are powerful
because we
have survived.

AUDRE LORDE

WHO YOU ARE
AUTHENTICALLY
IS ALL RIGHT.

LAVERNE COX

Be so completely yourself

To be afraid
is to behave as
if the truth were
not true.

BAYARD RUSTIN

MY HAPPINESS
GROWS IN DIRECT
PROPORTION TO
MY ACCEPTANCE
AND IN INVERSE
PROPORTION TO
MY EXPECTATIONS.

MICHAEL J. FOX

The first step to becoming strong is to decide that you are

Accept no one's definition of your life; define yourself.

HARVEY FIERSTEIN

TAKE THAT
BIG LEAP FORWARD
WITHOUT HESITATION,
WITHOUT ONCE
LOOKING BACK.

ALYSON NOËL

Let your dreams set sail

SOME OF US
THINK HOLDING
ON MAKES US
STRONG, BUT
SOMETIMES IT IS
LETTING GO.

HERMANN HESSE

Whoever is happy will make others happy too.

ANNE FRANK

Never trade your authenticity for approval

Destiny is not a matter of chance; it is a matter of choice.

WILLIAM JENNINGS BRYAN

Be yourself.
Everybody else is
already taken.

ANONYMOUS

YOU ATTRACT
THE RIGHT THINGS
WHEN YOU HAVE
A SENSE OF
WHO YOU ARE.

AMY POEHLER

Be bright
be bold
be you

If you're interested in finding out more about our books, find us on Facebook at **Summersdale Publishers** and follow us on Twitter at **@Summersdale**.

www.summersdale.com